25 BACH DUETS
FROM THE CANTATAS

FOR TWO CELLOS
(or any two bass clef instruments)

Compiled and Edited by
FRED SHERRY

ISBN 978-1-4584-0793-1

BOOSEY & HAWKES

DISTRIBUTED BY

HAL•LEONARD®

www.boosey.com
www.halleonard.com

Contact us:
Hal Leonard
7777 West Bluemound Road
Milwaukee, WI 53213
Email: info@halleonard.com

In Europe, contact:
Hal Leonard Europe Limited
42 Wigmore Street
Marylebone, London, W1U 2RN
Email: info@halleonardeurope.com

In Australia, contact:
Hal Leonard Australia Pty. Ltd.
4 Lentara Court
Cheltenham, Victoria, 3192 Australia
Email: info@halleonard.com.au

Thanks to Carol Archer for her constant support.
I am grateful to Michael Nicolas, Edgar Meyer, and my students for reading through the duets.
Special thanks to Mairi Dorman-Phaneuf, who prepared the original version for publication.

INTRODUCTION TO REVISED EDITION

Move around in *25 Bach Duets from the Cantatas* as you please; the order of the duets is not significant, though they generally trend from easy to difficult and traditional to esoteric. These duets offer an excellent way to study Bach's music, but you must learn both parts to get the full effect!

Aside from cleaning up some mistakes for this revised edition, I wrote music for Cello I to play during the rests that occur in all the duets except Nos. 1 and 25. This music is designed to take the place of what would be the right hand of the keyboard in the continuo section. Generally, the continuo section in Bach's music consists of a keyboard, cello and/or bass, and sometimes bassoon. In our time the right hand of the keyboard is played in a basic chordal style or in a manner that imitates the main theme of the composition. According to musicians who heard Bach play, his right hand sounded like a fully composed three-voice composition. My imagination tells me that it was a fascinating, original, and eloquent accompaniment of great power, pathos, and joy. I labored long hours over the new Cello I bits. When Bach did not provide a figured bass, I made up my own and channeled, as well as I could, the master's feeling for dissonance and resolution. I encourage you to study figured bass, the important set of numbers and signs that indicates harmonic action. It has been used by composers such as Purcell, Bach, Mozart, and Beethoven and is used today by performers of early music.

If you are playing the Cello I part, you can play the cue-sized bits that I wrote to replace the rests, or you can double the Cello II part. If you play the cue-sized notes, it is good to vary the tone color in a manner that separates them from Bach's notes. Players of other bass clef instruments such as bassoon, trombone, French horn, tuba, bass clarinet, and contrabass have found this book useful and gratifying. Some of these duets benefit when the Cello II part is played by a contrabass and read in the standard way. While I always had reasons for my suggested fingerings, it is your job to decide whether to use them or make up your own. Please do not worry about period performance practice, as Bach is the composer for all periods and styles.

Double dots were not yet used during Bach's time, but in this book they are employed in Nos. 5 and 19. Duets Nos. 8 and 9 are both in c minor. The original key signature of No. 8, two flats, has been preserved; in No. 9 it has been changed to three flats. This was done to acquaint you with the idea that the sixth step of the scale can be natural or flat.

The chorale tunes that accompany Nos. 16, 17, and 25 are included as an insert to this performance score. They can be played on any instrument comfortable in the treble clef: flute, oboe, clarinet, violin, viola…cello?

On a personal note, working on this book rescued me from drowning in the tidal wave of performers and editors past and present who have taken on the cello suites. Treasure this music, and if you need more, the 200-plus cantatas offer much beautiful and challenging cello writing.

Every day is practice day,
Fred Sherry

1. Why are you so fearful?

Cantata 81: "Ihr Kleingläubigen, warum seid ihr so furchtsam?"

J.S. BACH
Transcribed for two cellos by
Fred Sherry

2. Where can a poor man find help?

Cantata 25: "Ach, wo hol' ich Armer Rath?"

J.S. BACH
Transcribed for two cellos by
Fred Sherry

Cue-sized notes are additions by F. Sherry.

3. Fear not
Cantata 88: "(Jesus sprach zu Simon) Fürchte dich nicht"

J.S. BACH
Transcribed for two cellos by
Fred Sherry

Cue-sized notes are additions by F. Sherry.

4. I go hence
Cantata 74: "Ich gehe hin"

J.S. BACH
Transcribed for two cellos by
Fred Sherry

Cue-sized notes are additions by F. Sherry.

5. Strong champion
Cantata 31: "Fürst des Lebens"

J.S. BACH
Transcribed for two cellos by
Fred Sherry

*Bach did not use double dots (they had not been invented yet).
Cue-sized notes are additions by F. Sherry.

6. Do not forget to share

Cantata 39: "Wohl-zuthun und mitzutheilen vergesset nicht"

J.S. BACH
Transcribed for two cellos by
Fred Sherry

Cue-sized notes are additions by F. Sherry.

7. The World Is like Smoke and Shadows
Cantata 94: "Die Welt ist wie ein Rauch und Schatten"

J.S. BACH
Transcribed for two cellos by
Fred Sherry

Cue-sized notes are additions by F. Sherry.

8. Be comforted

Cantata 87: "In der Welt habt ihr Angst"

J.S. BACH
Transcribed for two cellos by
Fred Sherry

*Bach's key signature.
Cue-sized notes are additions by F. Sherry.

9. Striving
Cantata 122: "O Menschen, die ihr täglich sündigt"

J.S. BACH
Transcribed for two cellos by
Fred Sherry

*Bach used 2 flats in the manuscript.
Cue-sized notes are additions by F. Sherry.

10. Rushing wind

Cantata 92: "Das Brausen von den rauhen Winden"

J.S. BACH
Transcribed for two cellos by
Fred Sherry

Cue-sized notes are additions by F. Sherry.

11. My anxiety is in vain
Cantata 97: "Nichts ist es spat und frühe"

J.S. BACH
Transcribed for two cellos by
Fred Sherry

Cue-sized notes are additions by F. Sherry.

12. Powerful
Cantata 185: "Das ist der Christen Kunst"

J.S. BACH
Transcribed for two cellos by
Fred Sherry

Cue-sized notes are additions by F. Sherry.

13. My heart is frightened

Cantata 111: "Entsetze dich, mein Herze, nicht"

J.S. BACH
Transcribed for two cellos by
Fred Sherry

Cue-sized notes are additions by F. Sherry.

14. Exuberant
Cantata 37: "Der Glaube ist das Pfand der Liebe"

J.S. BACH
Transcribed for two cellos by
Fred Sherry

Cue-sized notes are additions by F. Sherry.

16. Think about him

Cantata 137: "Lobe den herren, der deinen Stand sichtbar gesegnet"
(Chorale Tune: Lobe den herren*)

J.S. BACH
Transcribed for two cellos by
Fred Sherry

*Played by trumpet in the original.

17. Be faithful

Cantata 12: "Sei getreu alle Pein"
(Chorale Tune: Jesu, meine Freude*)

J.S. BACH
Transcribed for two cellos by
Fred Sherry

*Played by trumpet in the original.

The original chorale tune is in a 4/4 time signature, changed by Bach.

25. The bright light
Cantata 6: "Ach bleib bei uns, Herr Jesu Christ"
(Chorale Tune: Ach bleib*)

J.S. BACH
Transcribed for two cellos by
Fred Sherry

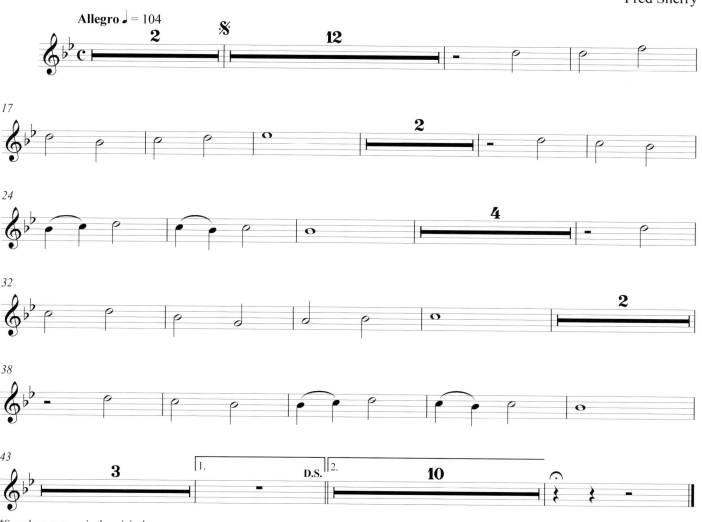

*Sung by a soprano in the original.

15. Hurl to the ground
Cantata 126: "Stürze zu Boden, schwülstige Stolze"

J.S. BACH
Transcribed for two cellos by
Fred Sherry

Cue-sized notes are additions by F. Sherry.

(switch parts on D.C.)

This page intentionally left blank to facilitate page turns.

16. Think about him

Cantata 137: "Lobe den herren, der deinen Stand sichtbar gesegnet"*

J.S. BACH
Transcribed for two cellos by
Fred Sherry

*See the insert for the chorale tune that accompanies this aria, included as an optional third part.
Cue-sized notes are additions by F. Sherry.

D.S.

17. Be faithful
Cantata 12: "Sei getreu alle Pein"*

J.S. BACH
Transcribed for two cellos by
Fred Sherry

*See the insert for the chorale tune that accompanies this aria, included as an optional third part.
Cue-sized notes are additions by F. Sherry.

(switch parts
on repeat)

18. He puts down the mighty

Cantata 10: "Gewaltige stösst Gott vom Stuhl"

J.S. BACH
Transcribed for two cellos by
Fred Sherry

19. Faith bestows the highest good

Cantata 129: "Gelobet sei der Herr, mein Gott"

J.S. BACH
Transcribed for two cellos by
Fred Sherry

*Bach did not use double dots (they had not been invented yet).
Cue-sized notes are additions by F. Sherry.

This page intentionally left blank to facilitate page turns.

20. Jarring
Cantata 76: "Hasse nur, hasse mich recht"

J.S. BACH
Transcribed for two cellos by
Fred Sherry

Cue-sized notes are additions by F. Sherry.

21. I feel anguish

Cantata 3: "Empfind ich Höllenangst und Pein"

J.S. BACH
Transcribed for two cellos by
Fred Sherry

Cue-sized notes are additions by F. Sherry.

22. Prosperity and trouble

Cantata 182: "Jesu, lass durch Wohl und Weh"

J.S. BACH
Transcribed for two cellos by
Fred Sherry

Cue-sized notes are additions by F. Sherry.

This page intentionally left blank to facilitate page turns.

23. Rejoice my heart

Cantata 21: "Erfreue dich Seele"

J.S. BACH
Transcribed for two cellos by
Fred Sherry

Cue-sized notes are additions by F. Sherry.

24. Listen and understand

Cantata 7: "Merkt und hört ihr Menschenkinder"

J.S. BACH
Transcribed for two cellos by
Fred Sherry

Cue-sized notes are additions by F. Sherry.

25. The bright light

Cantata 6: "Ach bleib bei uns, Herr Jesu Christ"*

J.S. BACH
Transcribed for two cellos by
Fred Sherry

*See the insert for the chorale tune that accompanies this aria, included as an optional third part.

CANTATA ARIA TEXTS & TRANSLATIONS

English translations by Fred Sherry

1. Cantata 81

Ihr Kleingläubigen, warum seid ihr so furchtsam?

You of little faith, why are you so fearful?

2. Cantata 25

Ach, wo hol' ich Armer Rath? Meinen Aussatz, meine Beulen kann kein Kraut, noch Pflaster heilen, als die Salb'aus Gilead

Ah, where can a poor man obtain advice? No herb nor plaster can heal my leprosy and boils except the balm of Gilead.

3. Cantata 88

(Jesus sprach zu Simon) Fürchte dich nicht; denn von nun an wirst du Menschen fahen

(Jesus said to Simon) Fear not, for from henceforth you will catch men.

4. Cantata 74

Ich gehe hin, und komme wieder zu euch. Hättet ihr mich lieb, so würdet ihr euch freuen

I go hence and come again to you. If you love me then you would rejoice.

5. Cantata 31

Fürst des Lebens, starker Streiter, hoch-gelobter Gottes-sohn, hebet dich des Kreuzes Leiter auf den höchsten Ehrenthron?
Wird, was dich zuvor gebunden, nun dein Schmuck und Edelstein? müssen deine Purpurwunden deiner Klarheit Strahlen sein?

Will he, the Prince of life, strong champion, God's son the highly praised, raise the Cross's ladder to the highest throne of honor?
Will what you previously cherished now be your adornment and jewel? Must your bruises become rays of clarity?

6. Cantata 39

Wohl-zuthun und mitzutheilen vergesset nicht, denn solche Opfer gefallen Gott wohl

If you are well off, do not forget to share, for God is well pleased by such offerings.

7. Cantata 94

Die Welt ist wie ein Rauch und Schatten der bald verschwindet und vergeht weil sie nur kurze Zeit besteht. Wenn aber Alles fällt und bricht, bleibt Jesus meine Zuversicht, an dem sich meine Seele hält. Darum, was frag ich nach der Welt!

The world is like smoke and shadows which soon disappear and dissolve as they only endure a short time. If however everything falls and breaks Jesus remains my confidence, and it is he on whom my soul fastens. Therefore, what do I ask from the world!

8. Cantata 87

In der Welt habt ihr Angst; aber seid getrost, ich habe die Welt überwunden

In the world you have tribulations; but be comforted, I have overcome the world.

9. Cantata 122

O Menschen, die ihr täglich sündigt, ihr sollt der Engel Freude sein. Ihr jubiliren des Geschrei, dass Gott mit euch versöhnet sei, hat euch den süssen Trost, verkündigt.

O men, you who daily sin, you shall be the angels' joy. Their jubilant cry is that God is reconciled with you, and has promised you sweet comfort.

10. Cantata 92

Das Brausen von den rauhen Winden macht, dass wir volle Ähren finden Des Kreuzes Ungestüm schafft bei dem Christen Frucht drum lasst uns Alle unser Leben dem weisen Herrscher ganz ergeben Kusst seines Sohnes Hand, verehrt die treue Zucht

The blustering of the rushing winds ensures that we will find a full harvest of corn. The cross's violence creates this fruit. Therefore let us completely surrender our life to the wise Lord, kiss His Son's hand and respect true discipline.

11. Cantata 97

Nichts ist es spat und frühe um alle meine Mühe, mein Sorgen ist umsonst Er mag's mit meinen Sachen nach seinem Eillen machen ich stell's in seine Gunst

Nothing is too late or early about all my trouble: my anxiety is in vain. He will fix my affairs at his own pace. I place myself in his favor.

12. Cantata 185

Das ist der Christen Kunst nur Gott und sich erkennen, von wahrer Liebe brennen nicht unzulässig richten, noch fremdes Thun vernichten des Nächsten nicht vergessen, mit reichem Masse messen Das macht bei Gott und Menschen Gunst

This is the Christians' art which only God and they themselves know, which burns with true love: which does not judge inadmissibly, nor destroy others' doings, which does not forget to mete out a rich measure to one's neighbor. This creates God's good favor to men.

13. Cantata 111

Entsetze dich, mein Herze, nicht Gott ist dein Trost und Zuversicht und deiner Seelen Leben. Ja, was sein weiser Rath bedacht, dem kann die Welt und Menschen-Macht unmöglich widerstreben

My heart is frightened without God, who is my comfort and confidence and my soul's life. Yes, His wise counsel provides for what the world and men would impossibly strive against.

14. Cantata 37

Der Glaube ist das Pfand der Liebe, die Jesus für die Seinen hegt

Faith is the pledge of love which Jesus cherishes for his own.

15. Cantata 126

Stürze zu Boden, schwülstige Stolze, mache zu nichte, was sie erdacht, Lass sie den Abgrund plötzlich verschlingen Wehre dem Toben feindlicher Macht Lass ihr Verlangen nimmer gelingen!

Hurl to the ground the arrogant proud ones and bring to naught what they have devised. Let them be swallowed suddenly by the abyss. Check the rage of their hostile power. Never let their desires succeed!

16. Cantata 137

Lobe den herren, der deinen Stand sichtbar gesegnet der aus dem Himmel mit Strömen der Liebe geregnet denke d'ran, was der Allmächtige kann der dir mit Liebe begegnet

Praise the Lord who has blessed your state. Think about him who has from heaven rained streams of love. Think thereon and what the Almighty can do for you who meet His love.

17. Cantata 12

Sei getreu alle Pein wird doch nur ein Kleines sein Nach dem Regen blüht der Segen, alles Wetter geht vorbei

Be faithful, all pain will then be only a trifle. After the rain blessings will flower and all bad weather will pass by.

18. Cantata 10

Gewaltige stösst Gott vom Stuhl hinunter in den Schwefelpfuhl die Niedern pflegt Gott zu erhöhen, dass sie wie Stern' am Himmel stehen Die Reichen lässt Gott bloss und leer die Hungrigen füllt er mit Gaben dass sie auf seinem Gnaden-Meer stets Reichthum und die Fülle haben

He puts down the mighty from their seats and thrusts them down into the brimstone pool. God raises up the lowly so that they can stand like stars in heaven. God leaves the rich destitute and empty and he fills up the hungry with gifts so that they who sail on His sea of mercy are always rich with abundance.

19. Cantata 129

Gelobet sei der Herr, mein Gott, mein Heil, mien Leben des Vaters liebster Sohn, der sich für mich gegeben der mich erlöset hat mit seinem theur-en Blut der mir in Glauben schenkt sich selbst das höchste Gut

Praised is the Lord, my god, my salvation, my life, the Father who has given his dearest Son for me, has redeemed me with His precious blood and through faith bestows the highest good.

20. Cantata 76

Hasse nur, hasse mich recht, feindlich's Geschlecht Christum gläubig zu umfassen, will ich alle Freude lassen

Hate only, hate me well Satan's minions, for I embrace belief in Jesus and I will abandon myself to his joy!

21. Cantata 3

Empfind ich Höllenangst und Pein doch muss beständig in dem Herzen ein rechter Freudenhimmel sein Ich darf nur Jesu Namen nennen, der kann auch unermessne Schmerzen als einen leichten Nebel trennen

Though I feel hell's anguish and pain yet I feel true heavenly joy when Jesus' name is mentioned, as he can scatter immeasurable pain like a thin cloud.

22. Cantata 182

Jesu, lass durch Wohl und Weh mich auch mit dir ziehen. Schreit die Welt nur "Kreuzige!", so lass mich nicht fliehen. Herr, vor deinem Kreuz-Panier Kron und Palmen find ich hier

Jesus, through prosperity and trouble You go with me. Even though the world cries "Crucify!" let me not flee. Lord, before your cross-banner crown and palms I find myself.

23. Cantata 21

Erfreue dich Seele, erfreue dich Herze, entweiche nun Kummer, verschwinde du Schmerze! Verwandle dich Weinen in lauteren Wein, es wird nun mein Ächzen ein Jauchzen nur sein? Es brennet und flammet die reineste Kerze der Liebe, des Trostes in Seele und Brust, weil Jesus mich tröstet mit himmlischer Lust

Rejoice my soul, rejoice my heart, banish sorrows, disappear pain! Can I transform my tears into pure wine and my sighs into exultation? There burns and flames the purest candle of love, the comfort of the soul and breast, because Jesus comforts me with heavenly delight.

24. Cantata 7

Merkt und hört ihr Menschenkinder, was Gott selbst die Taufe heisst Es muss zwar hier Wasser sein, doch schlecht Wasser nicht allein Gottes Wort und Gottes Geist tauft und reiniget die Sünder

Listen and understand children of men when God Himself designates the baptism. There must indeed be water here, yet not only water but God's word and spirit baptizes and cleanses sinners.

25. Cantata 6

Ach bleib bei uns, Herr Jesu Christ, Abend worden ist, dein göttlich Worte, das helle Licht, lass ja bei uns auslöschen nicht. In dieser letzt betrübten zeit Herr, Beständigkeit, dass wir dein Wort und Sacrament rein behalt'n bis an unser End'.

Ah, remain with us Lord Jesus Christ. Even though it has become evening your godly word, the bright light, will not be extinguished. In this last troubled time grant us, Lord, steadfastness, so that we keep your word and the holy sacrament until our end.

Published by Boosey & Hawkes, Inc.
229 West 28th Street
New York NY 10001

www.boosey.com

ISMN 979-0-051-10651-6
Printed in U.S.A. and distributed by Hal Leonard, Milwaukee WI
First printed 2011

REVISED EDITION 2019